I Learn to Trust God

Carolyn Nystrom

Illustrated by
Dwight Walles

MOODY PRESS
CHICAGO

© 1990 by
Carolyn Nystrom

Moody Press, a ministry of the Moody Bible Institute,
is designed for education, evangelization, and edification. If
we may assist you in knowing more about Christ and the
Christian life, please write us without obligation:
Moody Press, c/o MLM, Chicago, IL 60610.

ISBN: 0-8024-6173-5

Printed in the United States of America

1 2 3 4 5 6 7 8 Printing/DP/Year 94 93 92 91 90

The night is dark. I lie in my bed and open my eyes wide, but I do not see. I open my ears, stretch them tight against my head, but I do not hear.

I hold my breath so as not to rattle the silence. Then I hear a *click, click, click* against the outside wall of my room. I see a flitter of light. And I am afraid.

I burrow down inside my bed, squeeze my eyes shut, and cover my ears. Is a monster ready to grab me and take me far away to its strange home? Is a thief searching my house for some favorite toy? Is a wild animal hungry for supper — me?

I know that by morning—when the sun washes the dark corners of my room and drenches the trees outdoors with light, I'll wonder why I was frightened. I'll remember my hot stuffy breath under the covers, and I'll feel silly.

But at night, it is dark. And I am afraid.

Psalm 56:3-4

The Bible says that when I am afraid I can trust in God. I wonder what there is about God that makes Him someone I can trust.

God is good.
Psalm 34:8

God can do anything He wants.
Matthew 19:26

God loves me.
John 3:16

God is in charge of everything in the world.
Acts 17:23-28

God never lies.
Hebrews 6:18

God will never leave me.
Deuteronomy 31:6

God made everything.

Genesis 1; Psalm 115:15

God made me.

Psalm 139:15-16

God always was and always will be.

Psalm 90:1-4; John 1:1; Revelation 1:17

No one can know everything about God.

Romans 11:33-36; Job 5:8-9

God is perfect.

Psalm 18:30; Isaiah 6:1-5

God knows everything.

Jeremiah 10:6-7

God is everywhere—all the time.

Psalm 139:7-12

Isaiah 64:8; Romans 9:18-24; 1 Corinthians 4:6-7

But what is trust? And how can trusting God help me when I am afraid at night?

The Bible says that God is like a potter who takes a clump of clay and makes it into a beautiful vase to hold flowers— or maybe into a plain clay pitcher to hold milk. The pitcher and the vase don't say to the potter, "Why did you make me this way? I wanted to be something else!"

When I trust God, I let God make me into the kind of person He wants— no matter what happens to me. So even when I am afraid, I can trust in God. And if I can remember what kind of God He is, I am not quite so afraid.

Matthew 8:25-34; Matthew 10:29-31

The field near my house is full of wild life. In summer, orange tiger lilies bristle near the edge, their petals streaked brown at the lip. Birds flutter through the grass and trees, their feathers colored soft buff, and red, and blue, and yellow, and green. God made all this — each petal, each feather. God made weed seeds and bugs as food for the birds. And God brings rain to water the flowers. God takes care of what He has made.

God made me too. I don't have feathers like the birds. I

wear a sun-faded dress and scruffy sandals. And I don't
eat seeds and bugs. My family gives me food that I like.
My family is God's way of taking care of me. God knows
how many hairs are on my head. And He cares.

If I want, God will take care of me forever— even after
I die. Long ago, God sent Jesus to the world to take the
punishment for everything that I do wrong. Jesus died on
a cross for those sins. But then, Jesus came back to life!

He talked and walked and ate with the people who knew Him. Later Jesus went up into heaven to make it ready for everyone who trusts Him.

If I believe that Jesus did all this for me, I will try to please Him with everything that I do. And someday I will live in heaven with Jesus and all the other believers. God will take care of us there forever and ever and ever.

Proverbs 3:5-6; Psalm 118:8

    I like to do things for myself. I like to work on a hard school project without help from my parents. I like to

make my own breakfast. I like to choose what clothes I will wear and what I will do with my time. Someday I will work at a job and earn all of the money to take care of myself. But even then I do not want to forget God.

God has also put me in a family: Mom, Dad, Lewis, and me. My family teaches me what I should do and not do. And God has given me the church— other people who believe in Him. These people study the Bible together. They help me know what is right. Even when I am grown up, I will still want to be part of a church.

But no one is more important than God: not I, not my family, not the people in my church. God is most important of all.

God invites us to talk to Him. I can tell God anything, even what I would not say to anyone else. I told God that I was angry because Dad blamed me for losing a ball. But I didn't lose it. Lewis did! I told God that I was sorry that I did not help my mom clean up the kitchen when she wanted me to. I told God that I am afraid of lots of things besides the dark. I'm also afraid of big dogs, and strangers, and being home alone. I can talk to God about good things too. I told God how happy I was to run and jump in the first warm spring rain. And I danced a happy

barefoot dance just for Him. I can talk to God anytime about anything — because God cares how I feel.

The Bible says that we can ask God for things too — whatever we want. And if God wants to give them to us, He will. I've been asking God for a baby sister for a long time.

But God does not alway give what we ask. I had a baby sister once. Her name was Laura. She got very, very sick. Mom and Dad took care of her. Doctors and nurses took care of her. Over and over, I asked God to make Laura well. But Laura died. My mom and dad were sad for a long, long time. They still don't smile or laugh as much as

they used to. And even when they do smile, their eyes are sad.

I don't know why God did not make Laura well. But I know that God loves me and that God loves Laura. God is still taking care of Laura — even in heaven.

Psalm 8; John 6:68-69

God sees things differently than we do. God always was and always will be. God is everywhere all the time. God understands all the past and all the future. So God knows the answer to any question that begins, "What if...?"

I can't know that much. But I can know that God has some reason for not giving me another baby sister yet. So I will try to enjoy the family that I have. I will help my mom make cookies. I will help my dad fix our broken door. I will even try to get along with my brother. (But I don't like it when Lewis runs his toys over my puzzle.)

In heaven, our whole family will be together again. Then maybe I will know why God has not always given what I ask.

Matthew 7:24-27; Psalm 31:3, 14-15a

In the Bible, Jesus told a story about two men and two houses. One man built his house on a sandy beach. But when a flood came, the house fell apart and washed away into the water. The other man built his house on a strong rock. A flood came to that house too. But the rock did not move and wash away like the sand. The rock stood solid even when the flood lapped all around. When the flood drifted away, the house on the rock stood as tall as ever.

God is like that rock. Sometimes terrible things happen to people — even those who believe in God. But God keeps on taking care of them — and they can keep on believing in Him.

Genesis 50:20; Romans 5:3-5; James 1:2-4

God can take hard things and turn them into something good. That happened for a man named Joseph in the Bible. Joseph's brothers hated him so much that they dumped him into a pit. Then they pulled him out of the pit and sold him as a slave. They told his father that he was dead. But in his new home, Joseph told his brothers,

"Don't be afraid. You wanted to hurt me, but God used that for good."

The Bible says that God can use hard things that happen to make us more patient. Maybe because I miss Laura so much, I can be more patient with Lewis.

It's hard to trust God when bad things happen. I want Him to take all the bad away and make it good again. But God does not always do that. Instead He wants us to trust Him, even when we don't get what we want.

God told a man in the Bible named Habakkuk that his whole country would be torn apart. Animals would die.

Plants would die. People would be taken away as slaves. Habakkuk did not like what God told him. He was so afraid that his heart pounded. But later he told God, "If the fig tree does not bud, and there are no grapes on the vine, and the olive crops fail, and the fields have no food, if there are no sheep in the pens, and no cattle in the stalls — even then I will rejoice in the Lord."

We can ask God to help us keep on trusting Him as Habakkuk did.

Psalm 43:5; Romans 15:13; Psalm 40:3

The Bible says that trusting God brings us hope, peace, joy, and even a song. So when I feel sad that my family is small, I can still hope that we will have many fun days together. When it rains, I can still dance for joy. When I lie frightened in a dark bed, I can still feel God's peace. And I can sing a quiet prayer song to Him.

Every day and every night, I can trust in God because God is great. And God cares about me.